Under the Arctic Ice

Copyright © 2023 Line Renslebråten

Under polarisen Copyright © Cappelen Damm, 2018

All rights reserved. No part of this publication may be reproduced, stored in a retrieval system or transmitted, in any form or by any means, without the prior written permission of Fitzhenry & Whiteside except in the case of brief excerpts in critical reviews and articles.

Published in Canada by Fitzhenry & Whiteside
209 Wicksteed Avenue, Unit 51
East York, ON M4G 0B1

Published in the United States by Fitzhenry & Whiteside
60 Leo M Birmingham Pkwy, Suite 107
Brighton, MA 02135

Fitzhenry & Whiteside acknowledges with thanks the Canada Council for the Arts, and the Ontario Arts Council for their support of our publishing program. We acknowledge the financial support of the Government of Canada through the Canada Book Fund (CBF) for our publishing activities.

The publisher has received financial support for the English translation from NORLA, Norwegian Literature Abroad.

Library and Archives Canada Cataloguing in Publication
Title: Under the Arctic ice / Line Renslebråten.
Other titles: Under polarisen. English
Names: Renslebråten, Line, 1980- author, illustrator. | Chace, Tara, translator.
Description: Translation of: Under polarisen. | Translated from the Norwegian by Tara Chace.
Identifiers: Canadiana 20230155480 | ISBN 9781554555741 (hardcover)
Subjects: LCSH: Marine ecology—Arctic Ocean—Juvenile literature. | LCSH: Marine animals—Arctic Ocean—Juvenile literature. | LCSH: Marine plants—Arctic Ocean—Juvenile literature.
Classification: LCC QH95.56 .R4613 2023 | DDC j577.7/32—dc23

Publisher Cataloging-in-Publication Data (U.S.)
Names: Renslebraten, Line, author. | Chace, Tara, translator.
Title: Under the Arctic Ice / Line Renslebraten ; Tara Chace, translator.

Description: Toronto, Ontario : Fitzhenry & Whiteside, 2023. | Originally published in Danish by Cappelen Damm, Oslo, Denmark, 2018 as "Under Polarisen". | Summary: "*Under the Arctic Ice* combines facts with visually strong and colorful illustrations where the theme is the importance of preserving the flora and fauna in the arctic region." – Provided by publisher.

Identifiers: ISBN 978-1-55455-574-1 (hardcover)

Subjects: LCSH Arctic regions – Conservation of natural resources – Juvenile literature. | Animals – Arctic region – Juvenile literature. | Plants – Arctic region – Juvenile literature. | BISAC: JUVENILE NONFICTION / Science & Nature.

Classification: LCC G614.R467 | DDC 919.8 – dc23

English edition
Design by Jillian Doll
Translated by Tara Chace
Edited by Susan Hughes
Printed in Canada by tc.Transcontinental Printing

www.fitzhenry.ca

Line Renslebråten

UNDER THE ARCTIC ICE

Fitzhenry & Whiteside

Far to the north,
at the very top of the world,
is the Arctic.
Here lies ice and snow as far as the eye can see.
And between the ice floes?
The ocean appears dark and cold.

But down below, the Arctic Ocean teems with life.
Animals live in their own ecosystems
within the ice itself,
in the ocean water, and on the seafloor.
All this life is interrelated.
Each small world is within a larger world
in which all the creatures have found their places
over millions of years.

LIVING ICE

The Arctic's cold winter is called the polar night.
Now, day is as dark and cold as night.
In the cold, the ice grows thick.
Animals and algae living in the ice sleep.
They wait for the light.

When the spring sun finally appears,
much of the ice melts.
Sunlight provides sustenance to algae and bacteria.
These tiny creatures flourish.
They become food for larger animals,
such as krill and amphipods.

BETWEEN ICE AND SEA

Heading from the open ocean into the sea ice,
the floes grow thicker.
The ice compresses.
The ice floes float tightly packed,
until they cover the ocean.

The edge of the ice may be miles wide.
This area is called the marginal ice zone.
It rings the Arctic like a belt.

The ice edge shrinks in summer
and grows in winter.

ICE ALGAE
ALGAE

A slimy, green carpet grows inside and under the sea ice.

This is algae.
Ice algae are "the grass of the ocean."
They are a type of plant that lives in the ice.
Ice algae are important food for tiny animals living under the ice.

When the spring sun warms the Arctic,
ice algae multiply rapidly.
In just a week, one alga will become 64 new algae.

When winter comes and the polar night sets over the Arctic,
the algae don't die.
Instead, they freeze inside the ice.
Or they sink to the bottom of the ocean.
There, they can live under sand and mud all winter long.

PHYTOPLANKTON
PHYTOPLANKTON

Plankton is a word that means "those who wander" in Greek.
Plankton are tiny organisms that are carried
along by currents in the water.
They are as small as motes of dust.
There are two kinds of plankton: phytoplankton and zooplankton.

Phytoplankton are tiny plants.
They live near the water's surface because
they need the light from the sun to live and grow.

ZOOPLANKTON
ZOOPLANKTON

Zooplankton float with the current.
Some can swim a little themselves.
Zooplankton are the smallest sea animals.
You can see them clearly under a microscope.

Zooplankton can be small crustaceans,
such as krill, amphipods, and copepods.
They can also be small jellyfish or snails.
Or the eggs and larvae of larger animals.

Life in the sea is a chain of animals
that need each other.
Zooplankton eat the phytoplankton and
hunt other zooplankton.
Fish, whales, and seabirds eat zooplankton.
Seabirds and seals eat fish.

COPEPODS
COPEPODA

With the spring sunshine, new life begins in the Arctic.
Copepods colour the black ocean red.
They are small crustaceans, a kind of zooplankton.
The largest species grow to the size of a fingernail.

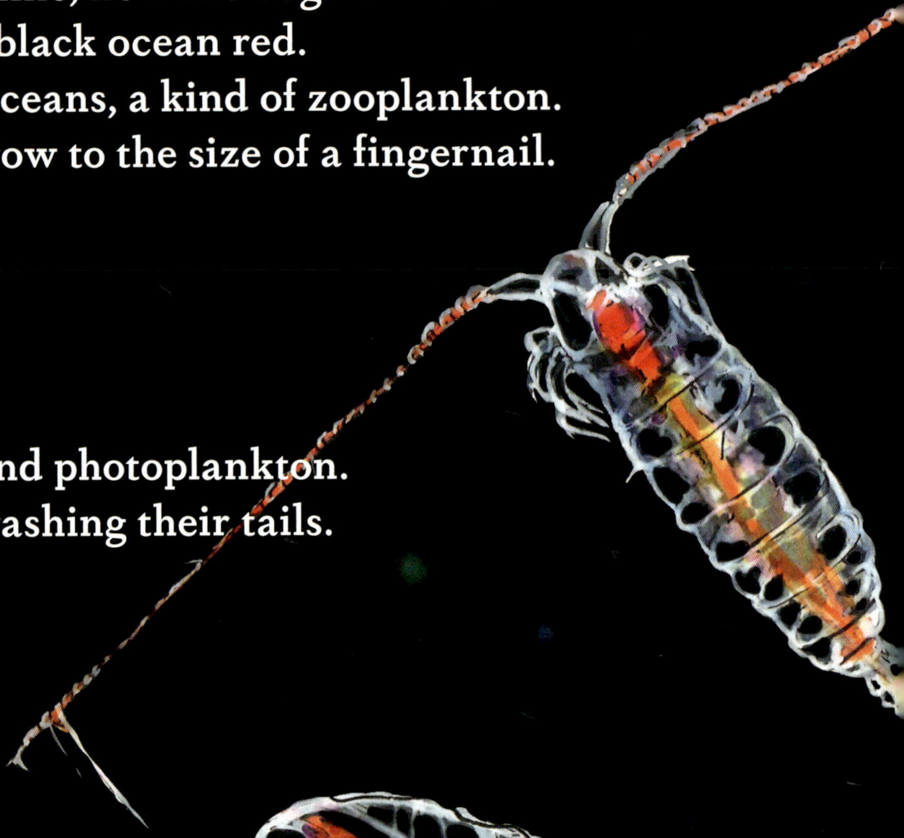

Copepods eat algae and photoplankton.
They can jump by thrashing their tails.

AMPHIPODS
AMPHIPODA

The ice is like a frozen city, full of streets and caves.
Amphipods thrive there.
They can grow as big as your pinky finger.
Amphipods graze on the algae under the ice.
They can also eat other zooplankton.

Some amphipods are called "beach fleas."
Why? Away from the Arctic, ampiphods usually live among
the seaweed and stones along the beach.
If you walk on the beach and pick up a stone,
they'll dance and jump around.
But in the Arctic, amphipods live inside the ice.
So maybe the amphipods can be called "ice fleas," too!

23

THE ICE IN THE ARCTIC

The Arctic Ocean has been covered by ice
for hundreds of thousands of years.
Some of the ice floating in the ocean is frozen seawater.

But some ice is made of freshwater.
Glaciers and ice formed on land are made of freshwater.
They are covered by snow almost all year round.

Icebergs are also made of freshwater.
In fact, they are the world's largest stores of freshwater.
They began as ice on land but
then broke off an ice shelf or glacier.
Now, that ice floats in the sea as huge blocks of freshwater ice!
Icebergs can be 60 metres [200 feet] high
and many kilometres long.
Only the tip of the iceberg is visible above the water.
Seven-eighths of it lie below the surface.

SEA ANGELS
GYMNOSOMATA

Small gelatinous angels glide through the dark water.
At night, the sea angels come to the surface to feed.
Sea angels are winged snails without shells.
They are no bigger than grains of rice.
These tiny predators
prey on other zooplankton.
When it gets light, the sea angels
sink back down to hide in the deep.

SEA BUTTERFLIES
THECOSOMATA

Sea butterflies are slightly smaller than sea angels.
Look—a snail-like foot with wings
sticks out of their shell.
When the sea butterfly wants to move,
it uses these wings as flippers.
Sea butterflies use a net of mucous to fish
for plankton and algae.
Sea butterflies change sex as they grow.
This is called being hermaphroditic.
They are males when they are young and small.
They are females when they become older and larger.

COMB JELLIES
CTENOPHORA

Comb jelly is a type of zooplankton.
The largest species of comb jelly can be as big as a hand.

Comb jellies have long ribs of hairlike cilia.
They use their cilia like paddles to move through the water.
But most of the time, comb jellies just drift here and there.

The comb jelly has no brain
but it's a predator that captures its own food, such as
other small zooplankton.
It coils its tentacles around the prey and guides
the food into an opening on its underside.

KRILL
EUPHAUSIACEA

Krill are found in all the Earth's oceans.
A swarm of krill can cover several miles.
Krill are zooplankton.
They look like shrimp—but they are half the size of shrimp.
Also, shrimp tails curl and krill tails don't!

In the Arctic Ocean, many creatures,
such as fish, whales, and seabirds eat krill.
Some need it to survive.

Krill hide in deep water during the day.
At night they rise to the surface of the water
to feed on phytoplankton.

If there isn't much food available, a krill shrinks its body size.
It does this to save energy so it needs less food!
A krill can survive for 200 days without food.

NORTHERN SHRIMP
PANDALUS BOREALIS

Shrimp live near the seafloor.
They eat plankton and small animals.
The shrimp have no teeth.
They rip up their food with their jaws.
Small grains of sand
in their stomachs grind up their food.

On average Northern Shrimp grow
to 5-10 centimetres (2-4 inches) in length
although some have grown
to 15 centimetres (6 inches) in length.

In the Arctic, shrimp can take seven years
 to reach adulthood.
They change sex as they grow.
Young shrimp are male;
adult shrimp are female.

FISH IN THE COLD

Fish need specific traits to survive in the cold Arctic Ocean.
No wonder only a few species of fish can live here year-round.
Examples are the snailfish, the snake blenny, and the eelpout.
But the Arctic cod is probably the most well-known of all the Arctic fish.

When the spring sun shines, other fish species come to visit the Arctic.
The most common are sculpin, haddock, capelin, herring, and wolffish.

Sharks are not bonefish.
Fish have skeletons made of bone.
The shark's skeleton is made of cartilage.
Cartilage is softer and more flexible than bone.
But some species of sharks also live in the Arctic Ocean.

The Greenland shark is a coldwater shark.
It eats seals and fish, and it can grow to be
more than 4.5 metres (15 feet) long.

ARCTIC COD
BOREOGADUS SAIDA

All winter long, tiny eggs lay hidden
in small caves and crevices
inside the sea ice.
The ice rumbles around the eggs.
They're waiting to hatch.
They will be Arctic cod.

As summer unfolds over the Arctic,
some Arctic cod head down to deeper waters.
Others stay behind, living in cavities in the ice.
If seabirds or seals pass by, the fish can hide
in these cracks in the ice.
Arctic cod eat amphipods
and small zooplankton stuck in the ice.

Arctic cod can live in very cold water—water so cold it's almost freezing. Antifreeze keeps the liquid in cars from freezing in the winter. Arctic cod have special antifreeze proteins in their blood to keep their blood from freezing, too.

SNAILFISH
LIPARIDA

The snailfish lies flat on the seafloor.
It sticks to a stone with a sucking disc on its belly.
It waits for its dinner to pass by.

    The snailfish is slightly smaller than the Arctic cod
    and looks a bit like a big tadpole.
    It has smooth, slippery skin and no scales.

There are many different species of snailfish.
One species is called the snot-fish
because the fish is so slippery and slimy.

SNAKE BLENNY
LUMPENUS

A snake blenny looks like an eel with spines on its back.
It rarely grows longer than a human hand.

Snake blennies hunt small animals and mussels on the sea floor.
They bury into the mud and lie there, completely still.
When they see their prey, they quickly shoot out from the mud to
catch it, and then bury themselves in the mud again.

EELPOUT
LYCODES

The eelpout also lurks
in the mud at the bottom of the ocean.
It has an elongated body.
Its head is wide and flat,
and it has dark markings on its skin.

The eelpout can grow to a length of 45 centimetres (18 inches). It preys on amphipods and starfish.

SO MANY TYPES OF ICE

Not all ice is the same!
Different conditions,
for example, different temperatures or different types of weather,
can create different types of ice.

Cold, choppy water can create pancake ice.
Pancake ice looks like round pancakes on the ocean's surface.

Hoarfrost are the ice crystals that form when fog freezes
on the cold surfaces of an object.

Amorphous ice is smooth, hard, and transparent. It looks like glass.
It is formed by the rapid cooling of water.

Did you know there is ice in space?
Most of it is amorphous ice, such as the rings of ice around Saturn.

THE SEABED

The bottom of the ocean is a place of colour and life—
starfish, sea anemones, and corals and more.
In some places, the seabed is hard and rocky.
In others, it is soft and muddy.

In some places, methane gas rises from under
the ocean bottom in plumes or columns.
The largest columns are as tall as skyscrapers.
Many types of undersea animal life gather around these columns.
They use the gas as a nutrient to live.

CARNATION CORAL
CAPNELLA FLORIDA

Carnation corals thrive where currents move the water. These corals are actually small animals that attach themselves to rocks and seamounts.

Seamounts are underwater mountains that rise from the ocean floor.

Corals are most commonly found in warm and tropical seas, but some species live in the Arctic, too.

SEA URCHIN
ECHINOIDEA

Sea urchins live on rocky seabeds and seamounts.
They belong to the group of animals called echinoderms.

Sea urchins eat kelp and seagrasses.
The mouth of the sea urchin is made of five
plates that form sharp teeth.

"The famous philosopher, Artistotle,
once wrote that the sea urchin's
mouth looks like the shape of a
lantern, so today it is known as
Aristotle's lantern."

SEA ANEMONE
ACTINIARIA

Sea anemones live on the seafloor.
They may look like colourful flowers, but they are animals.
Sea anemones can move,
but only very slowly.
They attach themselves to stones and shells with a suction cup.

More than 80 tentacles wave elegantly in the water.
The tentacles are full of poison.
Sea anemones use their tentacles to hunt their prey.
The poison in their tentacles stuns their prey
so it cannot move.
They can eat animals as big as they are!

Sea anemones have an opening called a "cloaca."
They use it for both taking in food and expelling waste.

FEATHER STAR
COMATULIDA

Feather stars are also echinoderms.
They start life as larvae
drifting around in the water.
Adult feather stars have featherlike arms.
A feather star can swim by raising and lowering its arms
or it can crawl along the seabed with the tips of its arms.
The small ring at the bottom of a feather star's stalk keeps
it attached to the seafloor.

SEA PEN
UMBELLULA ENCRINUS

Sea pens look like palm trees swaying.
The bottom part of their stalk anchors them
in the mud or sand.
Their body is at the very top of their stalk, and
their mouth is in the center of their body.
The sea pen's waving tentacles around its mouth
catch plankton drifting by.
Although sea pens look like plants, they are
animals and are related to corals.

WHY DOES THE ICE LOOK BLUE?

Sometimes ice looks white. But sometimes it looks blue!
Look at the beautiful turquoise and blue icebergs—
and the great expanses of white ice with blue shadows.

It's the light from the sun that makes the ice look white or blue.
The sun's rays emit light in all colours of the rainbow.
Blue light penetrates deepest into the ice
before it is reflected, or thrown back out.
Clear ice looks blue because blue light is reflected last.

Ice looks white when almost all of the light is reflected.

SEA SPIDER
PYCNOGONIDA

The sea spider, which can grow as big as a cat, almost looks like it comes from another planet.

With only a tiny body, it consists almost entirely of long legs. Even its internal organs are in its legs.

Sea spiders use their legs to move about and to breathe. After they mate with the females, male sea spiders carry the fertilized eggs on their legs until they hatch.

Sea spiders eat small animals on the seafloor. Here's how: they stick their proboscis into their prey—and suck out their bodily fluids.

ICELAND SCALLOP
CHLAMYS ISLANDICA

The Iceland scallop is a bivalve.
A Bivalve is a mollusk with a hinged shell.
The Iceland scallop can be ten centimetres (four inches) long.
It has bold hues of green, red, and yellow—
and is easy to spot on the seafloor!

GREENLAND COCKLE
SERRIPES GROENLANDICUS

The Greenland cockle is round in shape and light in colour. It burrows into the seabed and lives there.
Greenland cockles are the favourite food of many seals in the Arctic.

COCKLE
CARDIIDAE

Small, chubby cockles live on the seabed.
When they become adults and get their shells, they burrow down into the ocean bottom.
Both seals and humans eat cockles.

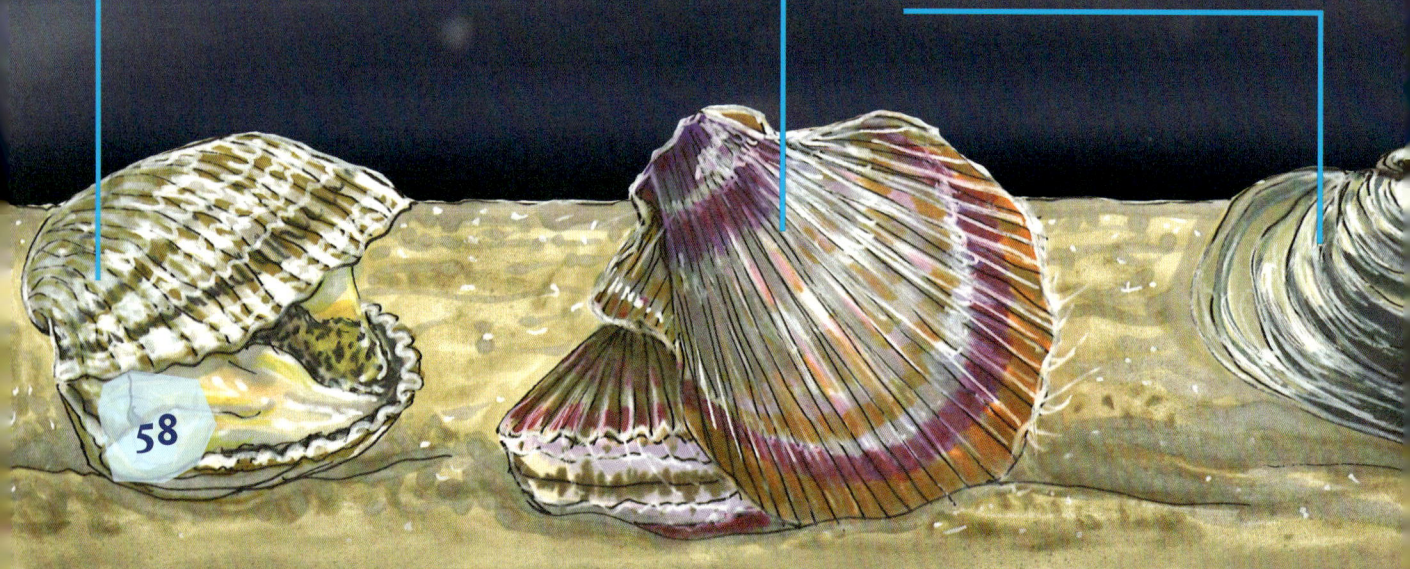

BLUNT GAPER
MYA TRUNCATA

The blunt gaper buries itself in the seafloor
and sticks its long trunk up through the mud.
It sucks in water and small bits of food with its trunk
and then expels the used water.

ARCTIC NUTCLAM
PORTLANDIA ARCTICA

The Arctic nutclam is yellowish-white
and elongated.
It can live to be over a hundred years old.
Did you know you can count the rings in a
tree trunk to find out how old a tree was?
Guess how scientists figure out
the age of Arctic nutclams?
They count the rings in their shells!

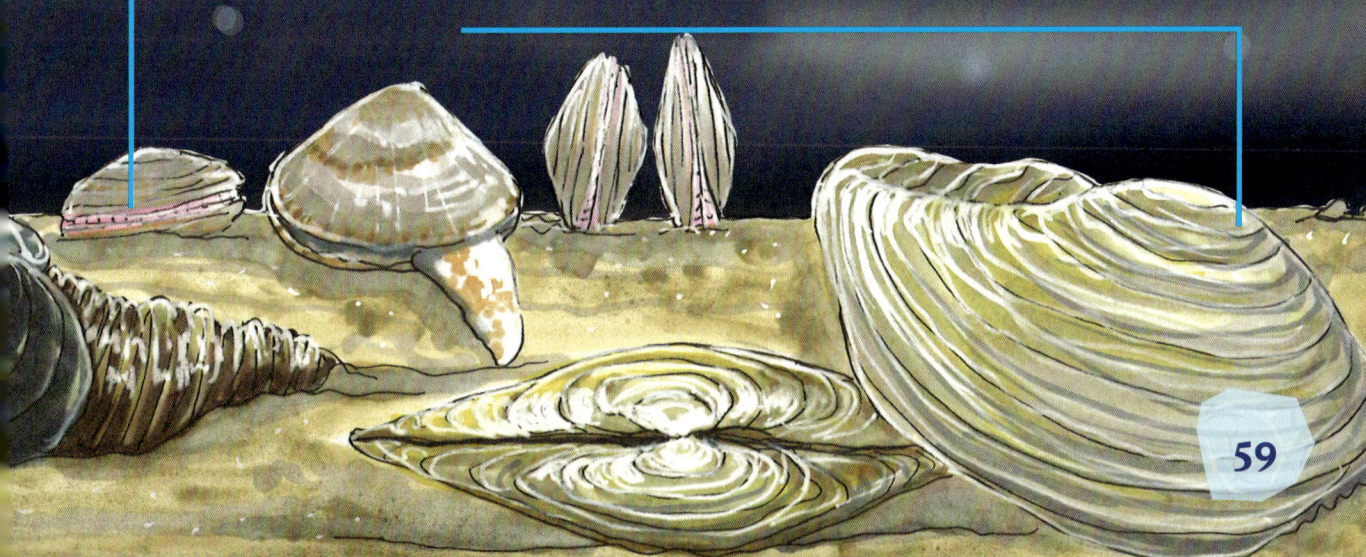

BRITTLE STAR
OPHIUROIDEA

The brittle star sits on the edge of a rock.
It is related to a starfish—but different.
A starfish has rigid arms which cannot move.
The brittle star can move its arms in any direction.
It uses its arms to move itself about and also to capture food.
The arms of the brittle star have small spines covered with mucus.
The brittle star waves its arms through the water
and traps plankton on the sticky mucus.

MUD STAR
CTENODISCUS CRISPATUS

There are many types of starfish at the bottom of the Arctic Ocean.
The mud star looks like a freshly baked cookie, with a comb of spines along its edges.
It lives underneath the soft mud.
It eats the sediment on the bottom and digests the organic matter.

BASKET STAR
GORGONOCEPHALUS

The basket star is a type of brittle star.
Its scientific name is *Gorgoncephalus*.

The name *Gorgonocephalus* comes from the word Gorgon,
who were monsters in Greek mythology.
A famous Gorgon named Medusa had hair of living snakes.

A basket star has five arms that branch off
into hundreds of smaller arms.
These arms are covered in tiny hooks and spines.
The basket star stretches out its arms
as amphipods and plankton float by,
entrapping and holding its food like
a spider catching flies in its web.

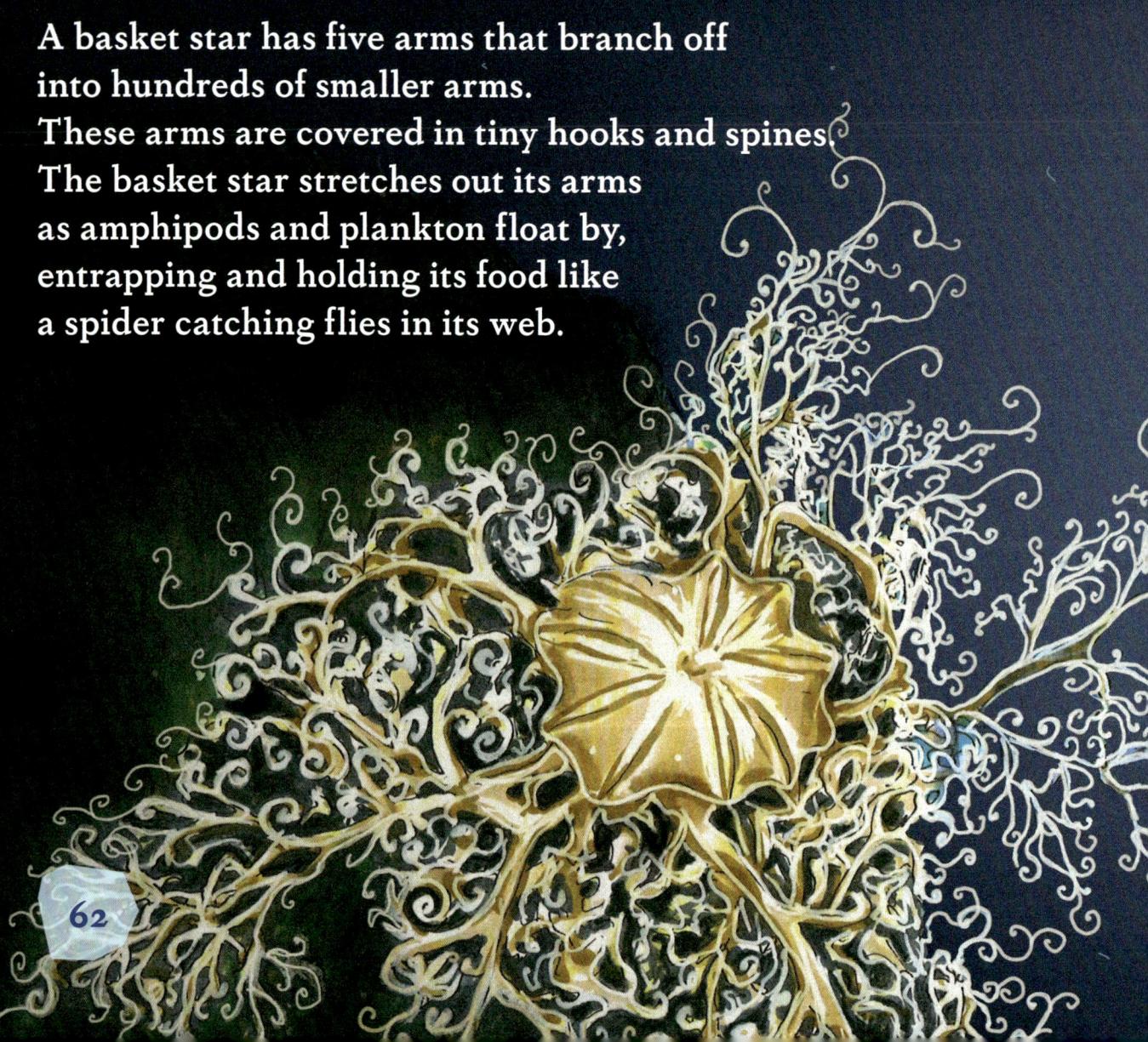

The basket star can measure up to 70 cm (27 inches) in arm length. When disturbed, it rolls up into a ball.

WHAT CAN THE ICE TELL US?

To find out how the climate in the Arctic is changing, we have to know what it was like in the past. Polar ice can tell us that.

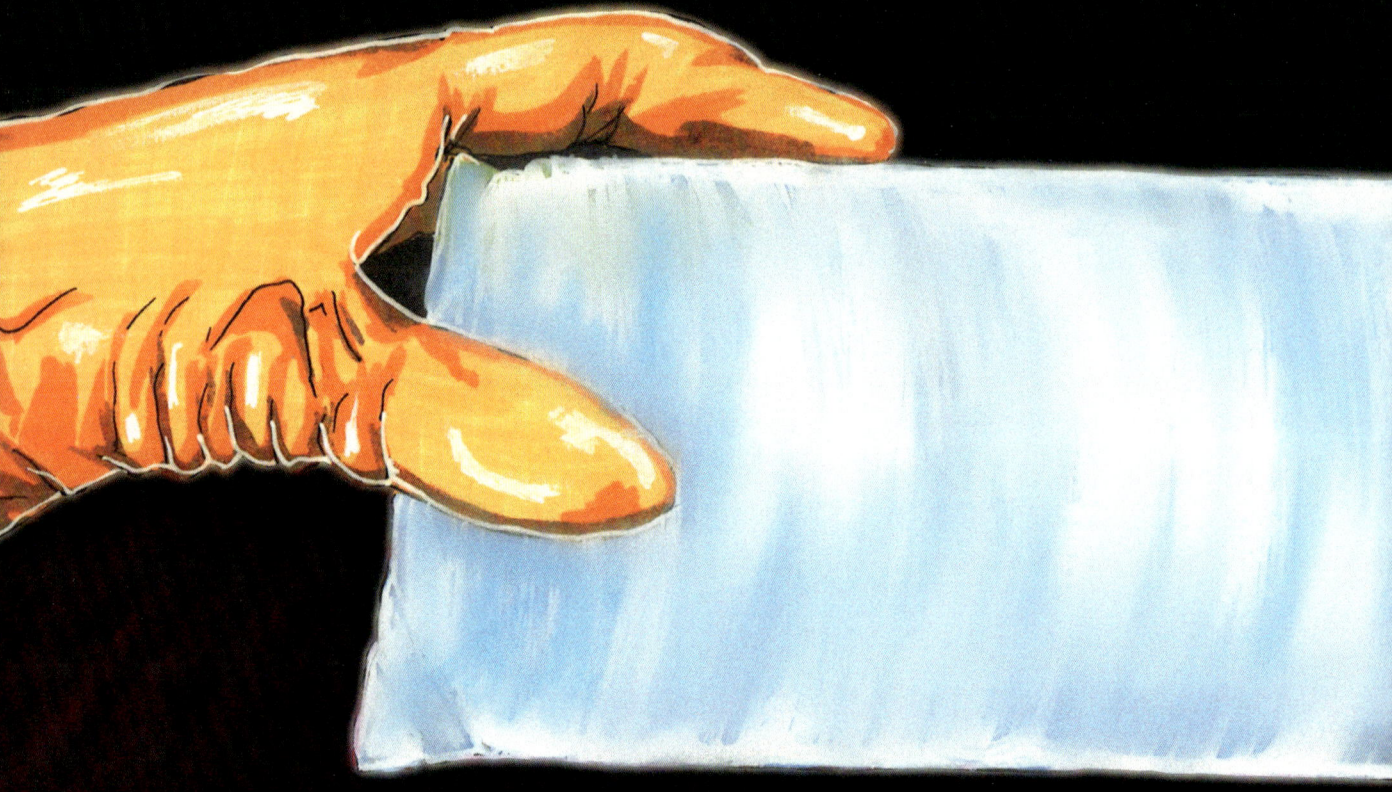

Scientists drill holes into the ice several kilometres deep.
They pull a long cylinder of ice out of the hole.
This is called an ice core.

Bubbles inside the ice contain ancient air from ancient Earth's atmosphere.

Scientists study this air to

In the ice core, scientists can sometimes see traces of volcanic eruptions and nuclear bomb detonations.

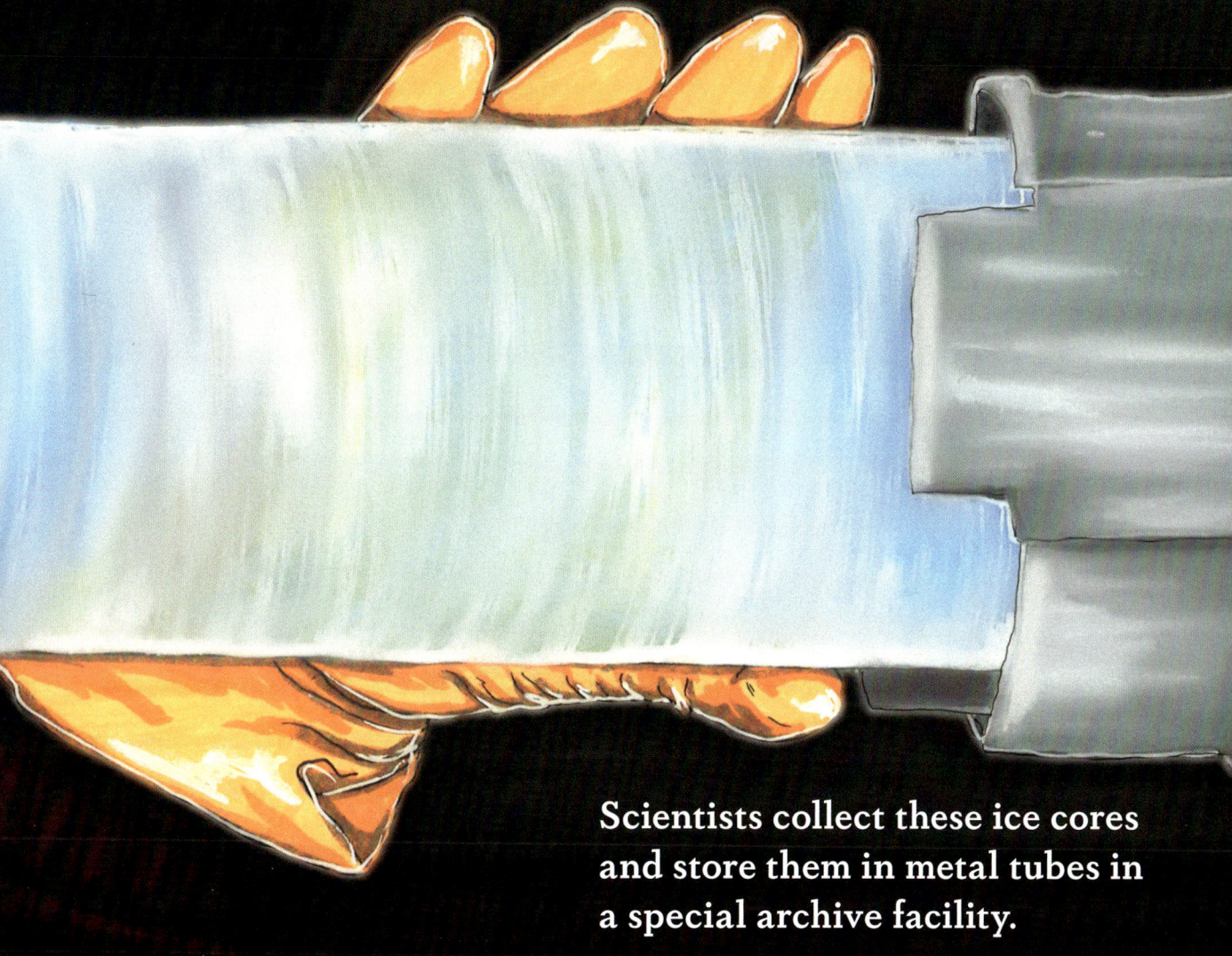

Scientists collect these ice cores and store them in metal tubes in a special archive facility.

65

MAMMALS IN COLD WATER

Mammals give birth to live young.
Marine mammals live most of their lives in water.
Seals and whales are marine mammals.
Polar bears are actually marine mammals, too,
because they spend more time on the
Arctic sea ice than on land.

Only a few species of seals and whales live in the Arctic year-round,
but many species come visiting.
Even blue whales will swim through on occasion.
The blue whale is the largest mammal on Earth.
It can grow to almost 30 metres [100 feet] long
and weigh 180 tonnes [200 tons].

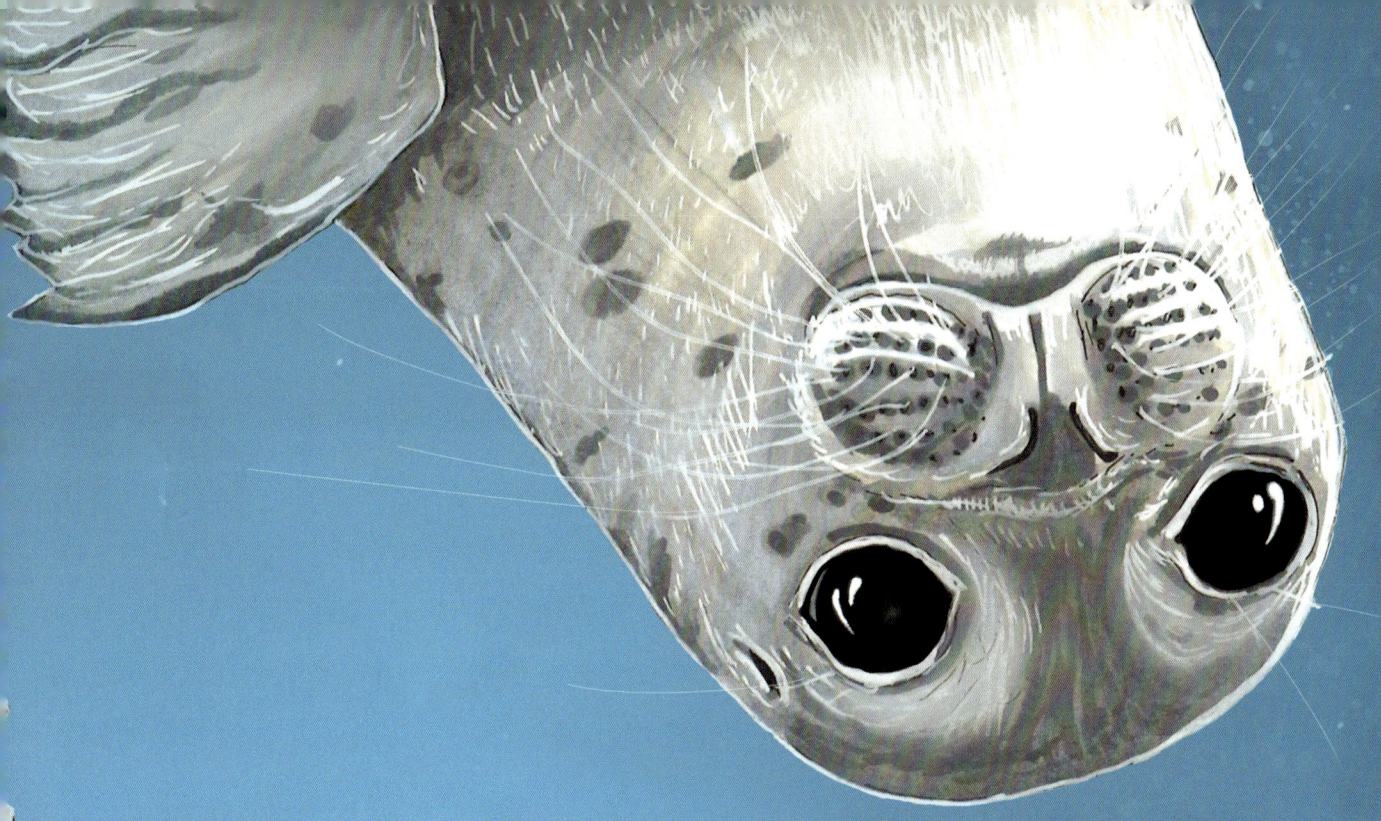

SEAL
PINNIPEDIA

In the Arctic, ringed seals and bearded seals live
on the sea ice year-round.
Seals come up onto the ice to give birth
and to molt into their summer coats.
Seals have difficulty moving on ice and land,
but they are amazing swimmers.
In the water they can swim, play,
and catch fish, such as Arctic cod.

Seals have a thick layer of fat under their skin called blubber,
that helps insulate them from the cold.

POLAR BEAR
URSUS MARITIMUS

The polar bear is the largest bear in the world.
It weighs about as much as a small car.
When standing on its hind legs, a polar bear
can be nearly 3 metres (10 feet) tall.

The polar bear hunts from the ice.
It eats mostly seals, but it can also eat fish, seabirds, and eggs.
The polar bear has a good sense of smell.
It can smell seals a kilometre (0.6 miles) away.

A polar bear's coat looks white—but it isn't. Each hair in the polar
bear's coat is actually a transparent colourless tube.
The hairs look white because they reflect the sunlight.
Under its coat, the polar bear's skin is black.
The black colour absorbs the maximum amount of solar radiation.
Polar bears can look a little yellow.
That's because they eat seals, and sea blubber has
high amounts of fatty yellow oil.

BOWHEAD WHALE
BALAENA MYSTICETUS

Bowhead whales can live to be 200 years old.
The largest Arctic animals, they are as long as two trucks and can weigh almost 100 tons.
A bowhead whale's head is enormous—
it is a third of the length of its body.

Bowhead whales eat marine invertebrates like amphipods and krill. Instead of teeth, bowhead whales have baleen. Baleen bristles look like a comb or brush. They hang down from the whale's upper jaw and act as a sieve when the whale eats.

The whale takes in a mouthful of water, and its baleen filters out the water while keeping the food in its mouth.

BELUGA WHALE
DELPHINAPTERUS LEUCAS

Sometimes sounds like the squeals and laughter
of children can be heard in the Arctic Ocean.
The beluga whales are talking to one another!
Because of these diverse and frequent sounds
the Beluga whale is often called
the canary of the sea.
The whales produce the sounds in the air sacs in their foreheads.

Beluga whales are dark grey at birth.
It takes almost eight years before they turn completely white.
Beluga whales can live up to 50 years.
They look small next to a bowhead whale,
but they can grow up to 5 metres (16 feet) in length.

NARWHAL
MONODON MONOCEROS

Long tusks stick up between the ice floes.
A pod of narwhals surfaces to breathe.

Narwhals are smaller than beluga whales.
They're called the unicorns of the sea.
Their tusk is actually a tooth that sticks out through their upper lip.
The tooth can grow up to 5 metres (18 feet) long
and narwhals use it to hunt fish.
They don't spear fish with their tusk, however.
Instead, they strike and stun their prey with the tusk and then eat it.

Narwhals live together in pods and
follow the shifting ice edge in the Arctic.
In the summer, as the ice begins to crack,
they swim into fjords and bays
to hunt fish, crustaceans, and octopus.

ICE WITH MANY NAMES

Ice belt, ice mosaic, iceberg,
old sea ice, freshwater ice,
summer ice, pack ice, drift ice,
brash ice, fast ice, floeberg,
growler, bergy bit, brinicle,
ice stream, ice island, hummock,
bummock, tongue, foot,
finger, ram, level, frazil,
grease ice, shuga, dark
nilas, sastrugi, polynya.

HOW MUCH ICE IS THERE IN THE ARCTIC?

When the polar night is over and the sun returns
in March, the polar ice begins to melt.
Then, near September,
the water begins to freeze again.
The amount of ice increases through the fall and winter.

Scientists have been measuring the ice in the Arctic for many decades
and they have discovered there is less and less of it every year.

In the past the shrinking Arctic ice may have been caused by solar
radiation, temperature, or wind.

But in recent years, pollution caused by cars and
factories has made the Earth's climate warmer,
causing the ice to melt at a greater rate.
This can potentially effect other ecosystems.
Rising water levels will threaten communities living close to the shore

THE ECOSYSTEM BETWEEN SEA AND ICE

In nature, everything is connected.
An ecosystem is a balance between living creatures
and the places where they live.
An ecosystem can be small like a pond,
big like a forest, or an enormous area like the sea ice edge.
The earth is an ecosystem, too, and so how
we humans live affects everything around us,
including the sea ice edge.

The sea ice edge ecosystem is vulnerable.
If the ice melts, algae and plankton disappear.
Fish won't have enough food
and their numbers will shrink.
If there are not enough fish, there will be fewer seals.
If the seals disappear, so will the polar bears.
The disappearance of one Arctic species
can ruin conditions for all other species in the Arctic.

ICE IS IMPORTANT FOR THE WHOLE WORLD

The Arctic is at one of Earth's poles.
Antarctica is at the other pole.
The ice in the Arctic and Antarctic
acts as the planet's own refrigerator.

The ice reflects the sun's rays,
making sure the planet doesn't get too hot.
If the ice melts, there will be flooding in many places.
In other places, there will be drought and famine.
Animals and plants may die out.

Unfortunately, the earth is getting warmer.
The earth is surrounded by a layer of air called the atmosphere.
The atmosphere protects us from radiation from outer space.
It also traps heat from the sun
which prevents Earth from getting too cold.
But the atmosphere also traps and stores harmful gases from
cars, boats, planes, and factories.
These gases are building up around the planet
and trapping radiation.
This is called the greenhouse effect.

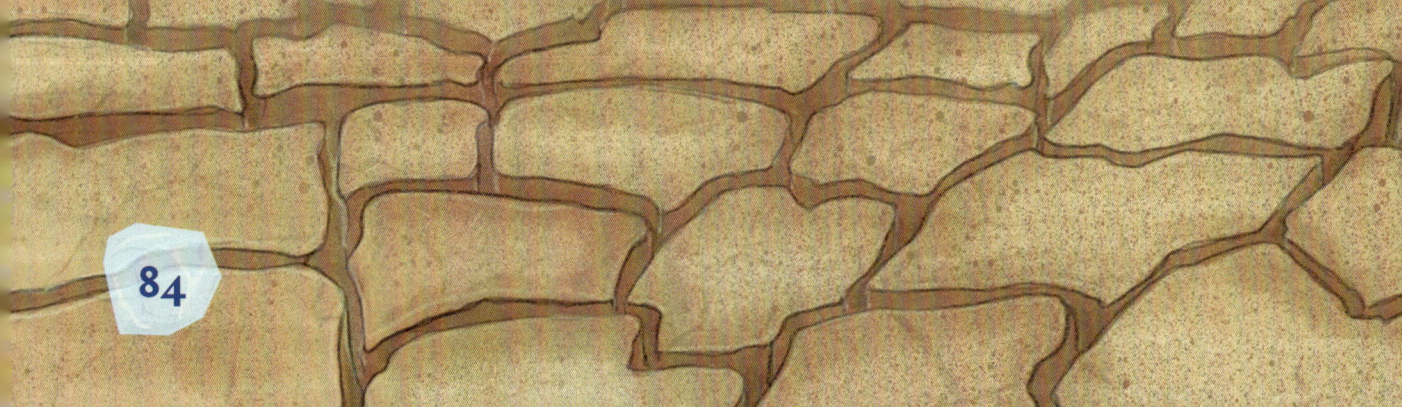

WHAT'S HAPPENING IN THE ARCTIC?

Because Earth is getting warmer,
winters in the Arctic are getting shorter.
The warmer temperatures in the Arctic mean
new species are coming to visit.
They may eat the food usually consumed
by the native Arctic species.

There is also less ice in the Arctic.
Because of this, large cargo ships can sail closer to the Arctic.
Ships can leak oil which can pollute the ocean
and harm the creatures who live there.
Because there is less ice, fishing boats go farther north.
Many pull large nets called trawl nets across
the ocean bottom to catch fish.
This type of fishing can harm the life
on the Arctic seafloor.

The plastic people use and throw away is also causing a big problem in all oceans, including the Arctic seas.

Every minute, 15 tons of plastic end up in the ocean.
In 30 years, there may be more plastic in the sea than fish!

Fish ingest tiny pieces of this plastic,
which can contain dangerous toxins.

The fish end up on our plates.

WHO'S PAYING ATTENTION?

Fortunately, many people care about life in the Arctic. Scientists use information from satellites flying over the Arctic to track the movement of the ice.
They study changes in the Arctic environment and work to find solutions.

But to solve environmental challenges, everyone needs to help. No one can do everything, but everyone can do something.

WHAT CAN WE DO?

Support organizations working to protect life in the Arctic.
> For example, you can support the World Wildlife Fund.
> You can adopt a polar bear!

Use less plastic.
> Use a reusable fabric shopping bag instead.
> Don't buy plastic straws, disposable cups, or utensils.

Walk or bike.
> Cars emit gases that aren't good for the atmosphere.

Don't throw away garbage in nature.
> Always take your garbage back with you when you go hiking or camping.

Ask, "Do we REALLY need to buy this?"
> The less we consume, the better it is for our planet!

Eat more food grown locally.

Eat more vegetables and less meat.
> Growing vegetables requires less of nature.

Don't prepare more food than you can eat.
> It takes a lot out of nature and the environment to produce food.

Recycle your garbage.
> Put paper into the paper bin; it can be made into new paper.
> Put plastic into the plastics bin; it can be turned into new products.
> Don't throw clothes or other textiles into the trash.
> Dyes in clothing and other textiles can contain environmental toxins.
> Instead, drop them off for recycling.

Throw away less.
> Try to repair what you already have, or deliver it to second-hand stores.

Travel less by airplane.
> Take the train instead. One flight from Oslo to London pollutes as much as driving a car for six months.

Join initiatives to clean your local waterways.
> Find local environmental organizations.

Tell others about what's happening to the environment, and share ideas about what you all can do!
Together we will make a difference!

A big thank-you for all the help to:
Lis Lindal Jørgensen at the Norwegian Institute of Marine Research
Elvar H. Hallfredsson at the Norwegian Institute of Marine Research
Philipp Assmy at the Norwegian Polar Institute
Haakon Hop at the Norwegian Polar Institute

Index

algae   8, 12–13, 18, 20, 25, 80
amphipods   16, 20, 34
    as prey   8, 34, 42, 60, 71
Arctic   5, 8, 11–13, 18, 22, 30, 34, 46, 56–57, 62, 65, 70, 72, 75, 78, 82, 84, 86
Arctic cod   32, 34–35, 36
    as prey   67
Arctic nutclam   57
Arctic Ocean   7, 23, 28, 32, 59, 65
Aristotle's lantern   47
atmosphere   63, 82

bacteria   8
basket star see brittle star
bivalve see mollusk
bottom of the ocean see seabed
brittle star   58, 60-61
blunt gaper   57

Carnation coral   46
cloaca   49
cockle   56
cold   33
comb jelly   27
    see also, zooplankton
corals   44, 46
copepods   16, 18
    see also, zooplankton
crustaceans, see plankton

ecosystem   7, 80
eelpout   33, 40–41
echinoderms   47

feather star   51
    see also, echinoderms

greenhouse effect   82
Greenland cockle see also, cockle
Greenland shark   32
Gorgon   60

hermaphroditic   25, 30

ice   8, 11–13, 43, 53, 62, 0, 76, 78, 80, 82
    amorphous ice   43
    floes   5, 11
    freshwater   23
    icebergs   23
    ice core   62–63
    glacier   23

hoarfrost   43
    marginal ice zone   11
    pancake ice   43
    polar ice   62

ice algae, see algae
Iceland scallop   56

kelp   16, 47
krill see plankton

mammals   65
methane gas   44
mud star see also, starfish
mussels   39

sea anemones   44, 49
sea angels   25
seabed   7, 14, 30, 40, 42, 44, 47, 49, 51, 55–57, 59, 84
sea butterflies   25
seagrass   47
seamounts   47–46
seals   16, 32, 34, 56, 65, 67-68, 80
sea pen   51
sea spider   54–55
sea urchin   47
    see also, echinoderms
shrimp, Northern   30
sharks   32
snailfish   32, 36-37
snake blenny   32, 39
snot-fish   38
starfish   44, 58-60
    as prey   42
sunlight   8, 53

phytoplankton, see plankton
plankton   8, 14, 16, 25, 28, 35, 51, 60, 71
poison   49
polar bears   65, 68, 80
polar night   8, 78
pollution   78

whales   65
    bowhead whale   70–71
    beluga whale   72
    narwhal   75

zooplankton, see plankton